Fly Wright

How to Pilot the First Wright Flyer

Christopher Felten

Copyright © 2023 Christopher L. Felten

All rights reserved.

ISBN: 979-8-9898267-0-4

DEDICATION

To my flight instructors Bryan and Alex who helped me become a good, safe pilot. And to my wife, Colette, who supports my many indulgences, kept dinners warm when instruction ran over and helped pay for it all!

CONTENTS

1	Getting to Kitty Hawk	1
2	The Wright Flyer – Preflight Inspection	5
3	Climb Aboard!	25
4	Cleared for Takeoff!	31
5	Bring It Home	39
	Epilogue	43
	1903 Flyer Specifications	49
	Glossary	52

~CHAPTER 1~

GETTING TO KITTY HAWK

"Man must rise above the Earth – to the top of the atmosphere and beyond – for only thus will he fully understand the world in which he lives" - Socrates

Your adventure to fly the first Wright Flyer begins in 1903 on a string of barrier islands separating the Atlantic Ocean from the mainland known as the Outer Banks of North Carolina. I hope you're not prone to sea sickness because before you can fly you must sail – in a George Washington Creef shad boat! These boats will not be equipped with engines until at least 1905, so sit back and enjoy the scenery.

Before arriving at Kitty Hawk, you stop briefly at Roanoke Island. Depending on where the crew docks that shad boat, prepare to hike about 4 miles south of Kitty Hawk to Kill Devil Hills. You pass by areas of short leaf pine trees, oaks, maples, cedars and cypress trees toward the Atlantic Ocean shore. Sand dunes rise one hundred feet or more. Kitty Hawk is a small fishing and farming community with only about 300 people and fairly well isolated from the rest of the world. There are a few homes, a United States Life Saving Station and a weather station… not too many structures to avoid on low altitude flights. This is a good thing… your Wright Flyer is not so nimble. In aviation parlance, it falls squarely into the category of "low and slow." And oh, by the way, you'll be lying face down with your head toward the canard style elevator in the front. Did you bring a helmet?

Orville and Wilbur Wright did not choose this area for your first flight by accident! In the same methodical way they approached every aspect of the flying machine, they wrote the U.S. Department of Agriculture Weather Bureau asking about suitable locations. A Weather Office existed at the Kitty Hawk Life Saving station from 1875 until 1904 to facilitate the repair of the telegraph line between Cape Hatteras and Cape Henry. A response came back from the Office of the Observer, J.J. Dosher:

Mr. Wilber Wright
Dayton Ohio

Dr. Sir,

In reply to yours of the 3rd, I will say the beach here is about one mile wide clear of trees or high hills, and islands for nearly sixty miles south. Conditions: The wind blows mostly from the North and Northeast September and October which is nearly down this piece of land. Giving you many miles of a steady wind with a free sweep. I am sorry to say that you could not rent a house here. So you will have to bring tents. You could obtain frame.

The only way to reach Kitty Hawk is from Manteo Roanoke Island N.C. in a small sail boat. From your letter I believe you would find it here like you wish. Will be pleased at any time to give you any information. Yours very respectfully.

J.J. Dosher

General Correspondence: Dosher, J.J. 1900. Manuscript/Mixed Material. https://www.loc.gov/item/wright002421

~CHAPTER 2~

THE WRIGHT FLYER – PREFLIGHT INSPECTION

"I fly because it releases my mind from the tyranny of petty things." – Antoine de Saint-Exupery

There it sits in the distance, disappearing and then reappearing again as you track up and down the dunes. You pull your coat tight and turn away from the freezing winds blowing off the Atlantic. As it comes into better view you start to wonder if this collection of spruce boards, bicycle wheel spoke wire and muslin fabric will keep anybody aloft! You're surprised it doesn't tumble away down the dunes on a gust of ocean breeze. It is a biplane of sorts with two large, stacked wings made of wood ribs running back to front connected by spars along the length of the wing and covered in white muslin. The sew lines of the muslin are pulled tight at a forty-five-degree angle all pointing like a large arrow toward the front of the wing over the frame. Canvas paint seals the fabric and makes it hard. The upper and lower wings are held apart by spruce struts and crisscrossed metal bracings made of bicycle spoke wire. The wings span 40 feet and 4 inches. The right wing is 4 inches longer than the left to produce slightly more lift and thereby compensate for the weight of the engine on that side.

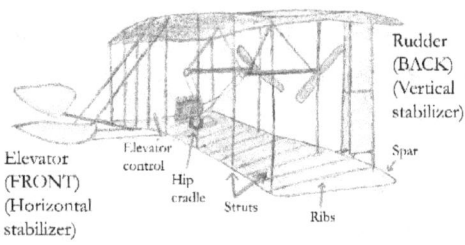

Before moving ahead any further we should define a basic aviation principle and some terms that will serve you well in preparing to pilot the Flyer. Assuming the operator is a safe driver and not a stuntman, carriages and automobiles normally move in only two horizontal dimensions. On a level surface this involves going forward, backward, left and right. This new flying machine on the other hand moves in three dimensions by adding a vertical component! By rotating around a lateral axis running from wingtip to wingtip, the nose and tail can be tilted up and down. This movement is called "pitch." Pitching up means raising the nose, which in the absence of aerobatics generally means pointing it toward the sky. You won't be performing any aerobatics in the Wright Flyer today... at least not intentionally and hopefully not at all.

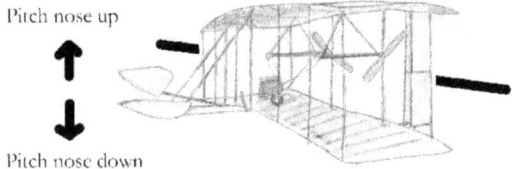

Lateral Axis

For the Flyer to turn, it must bank or roll left and right. This movement, called "roll," occurs around a longitudinal axis running from the front of the aircraft to the tail.

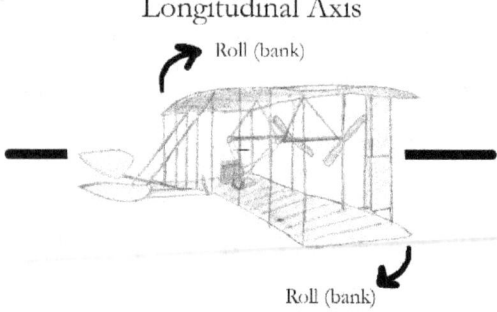

The last movement occurs around a vertical axis running from top to bottom through the aircraft's center of gravity. This movement, called "yaw," allows for the nose to move left and right in the horizontal plane. Like turning your car left and right in the road.

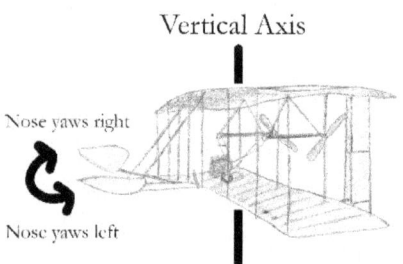

So, your Flyer will pitch up and down around a lateral axis along the wings, yaw left and right around a vertical axis from top to bottom, and the wings will roll around a longitudinal axis running from the front elevator to the rear rudders. Pitch is used when climbing and descending, though engine power also plays a large role in those maneuvers. In fact, unless you force the nose to pitch down, just adding engine power alone will cause an airplane to climb just as you would expect a lack of power would start a descent. Hence the real danger of an engine failure! Roll is necessary to bank and turn the aircraft. Yaw your nose into the wind to keep a straight line along the ground when wind starts to blow you off course. But yaw the nose back and straight with the runway when you land so you don't touch-down at an angle – a potentially dangerous mistake called "side-loading" the aircraft.

Lift to keep you and your Flyer aloft is created by wind flowing over those two glorious wood and fabric wings. The two components of lift are traditionally described by Bernoulli's theorem and Newton's third law. Daniel Bernoulli stated in the eighteenth century that as the velocity of a fluid (or air) increases, its pressure decreases. The top curvature or camber of the Wright Flyer wing forces the air to move more quickly over the top of the wing than the flatter bottom. According to Bernoulli, this creates a pressure differential between the top and the bottom, lifting the wing. In addition, Newton's third law states that for every action there is an equal and opposite reaction. As the air passes over the curved wing, it is bent to create a downward force off the trailing edge. The equal and opposite force creates lift that adds to Bernoulli's pressure differential and up the wing goes; And hopefully the Flyer along with it! There is some disagreement over which principle plays the greater role in lift – Bernoulli's theorem or Newton's third law. These squabbles over physics aside, there are several agreed upon factors that influence lift.

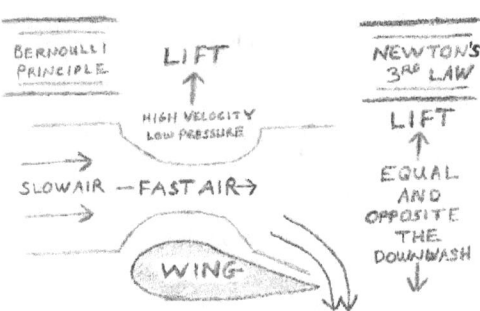

Area: The larger the area of the wing, the more lift will be created. Of course, a larger wing will also be heavier and harder to lift!

Velocity (speed) of wind over the wing: The higher the velocity, the greater the lift. That stiff ocean breeze will work in our favor to lift away from the sand.

Air density: The amount of air molecules in a given volume varies with pressure, temperature and humidity. Since pressure and air density decrease with altitude, Kitty Hawk, N.C. at sea level is a good place to fly – the air is dense. Density also decreases at higher temperatures. Density altitude is the pressure altitude corrected for temperature. The formula for density altitude is Density Altitude in feet = Pressure Altitude in feet + (120 x (Outside Air Temperature Celsius – Standard Temperature Celsius)). It is often thought of as the altitude the airplane "feels" based on performance. High temperatures mean lower pressure and higher density altitude which translates into less lift. For instance, the altitude of Kitty Hawk, North Carolina is only 7 feet. On a day where the pressure is standard (29.92 Hg) and the temperature is standard (15C or 59F) the airplane would perform like it was at a true altitude of 7 feet. However, if the pressure is standard, but it is a warm summer day in Kitty Hawk, such as 29C (85F) then the airplane performs as if it is taking off at a density altitude of 7 feet + (120 x (29C – 15C)) which computes to 1687 feet! Tighten your scarf and turn your back to the cold biting wind. It is in the mid-thirties Fahrenheit at Kill Devil Hills today, making high density altitude due to soaring temperatures a nonissue! In fact, the formula shows the benefit of being even colder than standard temperature this time of year: 7 feet + (120 x (1.7C − 15C)) which computes to 1589 below sea level (-1589 feet)! Now that is dense air! So, the Wright brothers picked an excellent spot for wings to develop lift − very dense air at sea level that is very cold and very windy. These are two really smart guys that started out building bicycles for a living!

Coefficient of Lift (CL): This coefficient takes into consideration the angle of attack − the angle between the chord line running from the leading edge to the trailing edge and the relative direction of the wind toward the wing. Lift will increase with an increasing angle of attack until the critical angle of attack is reached. At this point the airflow over the wing becomes disorganized and turbulent and breaks away from the wing surface. The wing abruptly loses lift and you start to fall toward the dunes… head first mind you! We'll cover that more in the cockpit. For now, suffice it to say that you never want to have to pull the nose up higher than the critical angle of attack to keep the Flyer aloft! We call this a stall at which time the nose will drop back down toward the sand regardless of how hard you pull back on the elevator control! In an abrupt and severe stall at low altitude there might not be enough time to regain lift before you create your own sand crater bringing a quick and possibly painful end to your flight! The lesson – don't pull back abruptly or too far on the elevator control!

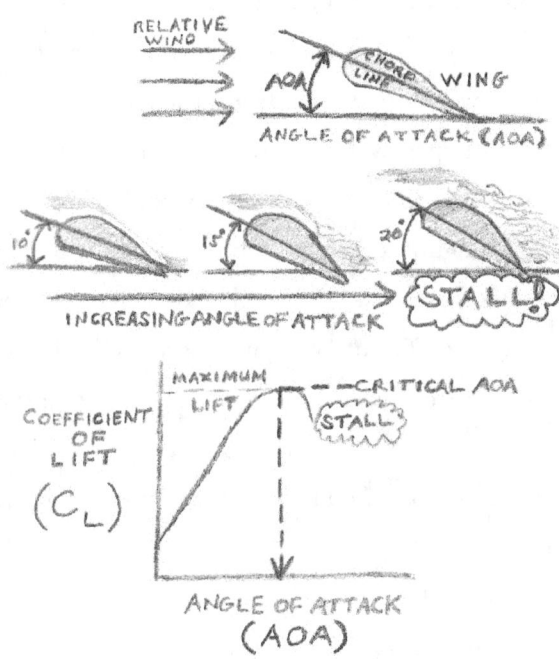

Here is the formula the Wright brothers used for lift (L): **L = k*V² *S*cL**

L = Lift
k = Smeaton's coefficient
V = Relative velocity of air over the wing
S = Wing area in square feet
cL = Coefficient of lift

Smeaton's coefficient (k) is a mathematical constant developed by John Smeaton in the mid-eighteenth century. It was a multiplying factor used in formulas to calculate lift specifically in air. Through their love of scientific discovery and relentless pursuit of accurate data, the Wright brothers performed studies with wing models in a small wind tunnel and discovered that Smeaton's coefficient was incorrect! The correct average value for the coefficient was 0.0033 rather than the 0.005 they were using from Smeaton's table! Their lift calculations based on his coefficient were off by 40-50%!

The lift formula shows us that lift is directly related to the area of the wing (S) and coefficient of lift (cL) and the square of the wind velocity over the wing (V^2). As a square in the formula, wind is clearly an important factor in lift. And while that cold, strong headwind is sure to numb your face making it difficult to talk, just remember, it's good for flying!

On the morning of December 17, 1903 we could use the following values in the formula:

k = 0.0033 (Corrected coefficient from the Wright brothers wind tunnel experiments)
V = 33.8 mph (27 mph headwind plus the groundspeed of the Wright Flyer of 6.8 mph – engine full out!)
S = 510 square feet
cL = 0.151 (from the Wright brothers table of lift coefficients)

Lift = $(0.0033)*(33.8)^2*(510)*(0.515)$ = 990 pounds

As every good pilot knows, weight and balance must be calculated prior to leaving the ground! We know the approximate lift produced will be 990 pounds. The basic empty weight of the Flyer with fuel and oil is 605 pounds. That gives us the potential to lift 385 pounds for the given conditions. You most definitely will not need luggage for this trip, and no one is volunteering as a passenger on your first attempt as Wright Flyer PIC (Pilot in Command)! Since this is only a make-believe flight, you can keep this answer to yourself... Will you get off the ground?

With that settled, turn your attention back to the preflight inspection. Looking at this beautiful machine more closely, one might wonder which end's the nose and which end's the tail? The elevator and rudder sit on opposite sides of the wing! I know what you're thinking – if I must lay on my stomach to fly this thing, I want to make sure I don't start down the launch skid feet first! The forward elevator became known as a canard design and despite being present on the first powered, heavier-than-air flying machine in 1903, it wasn't mass produced until the Saab Viggen jet fighter in 1967!

More modern planes have the horizontal stabilizer and elevators in the back tail or "empennage" section. Because single engine, propeller driven airplanes tend to have a forward center of gravity that makes them nose heavy, the horizontal stabilizers of the tail create a downward balancing force to keep the airplane level along its lateral axis. While this stabilizes the pitch of the airplane, it comes at a cost. The wing now must provide enough lift for both the weight of the airplane, fuel and passengers plus the horizontal stabilizer's downward force. The Wright Flyer canard design puts the horizontal stabilizer in the front to act as a small wing providing the lift necessary to keep the nose up. This is now adding to the total lift of the Flyer rather than subtracting like it does when the horizontal stabilizer is in the back. Orville wrote in a letter many years later to Alexander Klemin on April 24, 1924, that they realized a rear elevator was more stable but "we retained the elevator in front for many years because it absolutely prevented a nose dive such as that in which Lilienthal and many others since have met their deaths." So, the brother's main reason for keeping the canard design was their idea that it better protected them from a catastrophic stall. The horizontal stabilizers in the front of the Wright Flyer also serve as the elevator to control pitch of the Flyer – pointing the nose up or down. The Wright Flyer model AB transition in 1910 added a horizontal stabilizer behind the rudders in the back followed then by a controllable elevator. Within the same year they were able to completely remove the front canard style stabilizer and elevator, creating the model B. This more resembled the airplanes of today.

Fly Wright

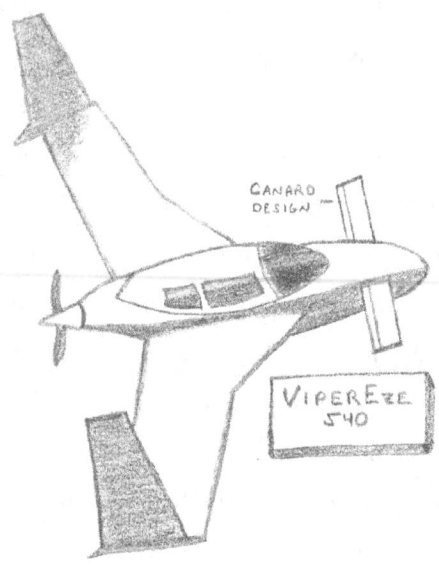

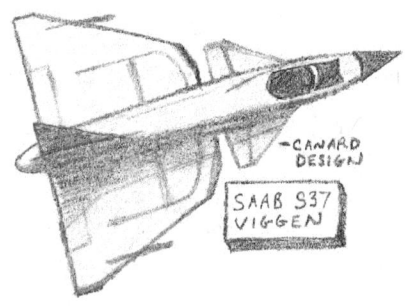

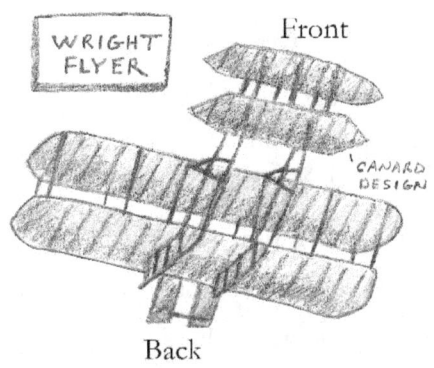

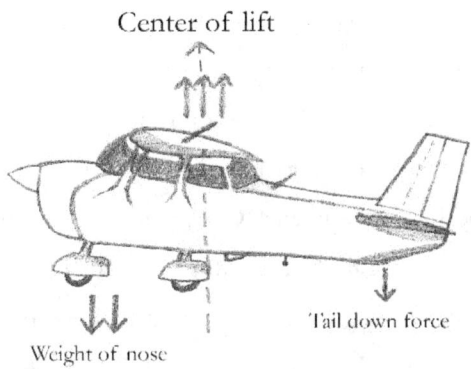

As you move around the Flyer, you will probably notice that the wings droop downward a bit; quite different from the up-sloping dihedral of modern, small aircraft. Keep this in mind as you take flight, because it makes the roll of the aircraft from left to right along the longitudinal axis less stable. It allows the wing to dip one way or the other more easily than modern airplanes that have upward tilting wings (dihedral). Forget about practicing 45- or 60-degree steep turns in the Wright Flyer! Make slow, gentle banking turns. Dihedral or upslope wings stabilize roll. As one wing dips and the other rises, the airplane starts to slip down sideways. The new direction of the relative wind gives the low wing a better angle of attack, which corrects the dip, returning the airplane to level flight. When the wings are drooping or anhedral, the opposite occurs. When the wing dips and sideslip occurs on anhedral wings, the higher wing gains more lift and the airplane rolls over even further – something to consider when one side of the Flyer wing starts to drop on you. Correct smoothly but quickly! Going into 1905, the Wright brothers caught on to this and stiffened the wing support rigging to give it a slight dihedral position and make it less likely to abruptly roll or bank left or right.

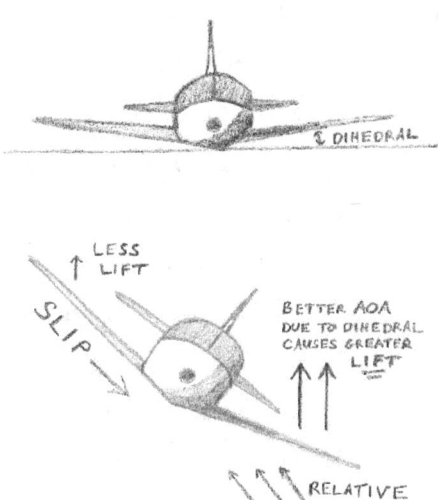

The back of the Flyer has twin, parallel rudders (vertical stabilizers) that are attached by cables to the wings. There is no horizontal stabilizer in the back.

Two long, thin propellers are connected behind each wing facing toward the back to push the Flyer. This is different than many modern aircraft that have a single propeller in the front to pull the airplane forward and force air over the wings and tail. They positioned the propellers in the rear out of concern that placing them in front to pull the Flyer could produce turbulent air over the wings. Of course, the Wright brothers designed a propeller to work with their machine. Many designers experimenting with flight at that time fashioned propellers after windmill or boat propellers. They were thick and heavy and inefficient at biting and moving air. The Wrights conceptualized propellers as just another wing developing lift in a horizontal fashion called thrust! Using their wind tunnel experiments, they developed propellers that were thinner, lighter and shaped to maximize this transfer of energy from the engine into thrust to propel the Flyer forward thereby pushing air over the wings. The two propellers convert about 66 percent of the mechanical energy from the engine to produce a combined thrust of 120 – 130 pounds at 330 revolutions per minute (RPM).

You might notice the chain connecting the engine to the far propeller is twisted so that the left propeller spins the opposite direction of the right. While it required carving two different propellers, this was another great idea by the Wright brothers to cancel out the effect of gyroscopic precession and torque. Thinking about Sir Isaac Newton again, he stated that every action has an equal and opposite reaction. If a propeller spins one direction, the airplane it is attached to wants to spin the opposite direction! By the Wright Flyer propellers spinning opposite directions, that tendency is cancelled out. Gyroscopic precession is slightly more complicated. Any spinning disc acts as a gyroscope and resists being twisted – it tends to be rigid in space. This is great for use in flight instruments and for balancing two-wheeled Segways, but not for controlling a light airplane in all three dimensions of open air! If an outside force is applied to a spinning disc, a responsive force is felt 90 degrees in the direction of the spin. Flying straight and level will not put any force on the gyroscope propeller. But you'll eventually pitch up to gain altitude and down to lose altitude. Pitching up will place a force on the top and bottom of that spinning propeller and that force will be felt 90 degrees around, pushing the airplane right or left. Again, having those large propellers spinning opposite directions should negate the effect of gyroscopic precession by the forces from each propeller acting exactly opposite to one another. Once again, those Wright brothers thought of everything!

What is spinning those long wooden propellers? Feast your eyes on yet another novel piece of machinery. Engines of the day did not meet the strict specifications of power and light weight needed to generate sufficient lift. The Wrights designed and built the Flyer's reciprocating gasoline powered internal combustion engine to fit their specific requirements of flight. They calculated the need for at least 8 horsepower in an engine that weighed no more than 200 pounds. It contains four cylinders and works similarly to a typical four-stroke engine. To make it less than 200 pounds, they built it out of aluminum with a small amount of copper – a first for the time. The body is cast aluminum, and the pistons are cast iron. The engine before you weighs only 180 pounds and can put out 12 horsepower at 1,025 revolutions per minute (RPM). They painted it all black to help conceal the material from competitors. Ah, early methods of protecting intellectual property!

~CHAPTER 3~

CLIMB ABOARD!

"Sometimes, flying feels too God-like to be attained by man. Sometimes, the world from above seems too beautiful, too wonderful, too distant for human eyes to see" – Charles A. Lindbergh

It is probably easiest to crouch down and enter at the front, just behind the canard style elevator, then lay on your stomach and stretch your feet back to the small wooden footrest near the back of the lower wing. Get your hips tucked tight into that cradle. While there's a lever connected to the elevator to control pitch, there is no yoke or flight stick here – you'll need to swivel your hips to bank, turn and steer!

There are some instruments up and to your

right side. Well, okay, up and to your right and behind you! No attitude or horizontal situation indicator. You have the real horizon for that – visual flight rules (VFR) only in the Wright Flyer! No altimeter! You can guess your altitude since you're facing the ground lying prone anyway. No compass either! Just takeoff into the wind and stay local for today. But you do have an anemometer to measure the wind speed, a stopwatch and a tachometer for the engine!

Orville and Wilber Wright borrowed the anemometer from a retired engineer named Octave Chanute. He was a Paris born engineer that lived in the United States and spent most of his retirement researching and writing about flight. He published a book in 1894, <u>Progress in Flying Machines</u>, which the Wright brothers used. He offered to let the Wright brothers borrow one of two portable anemometers he owned so they could measure wind velocity. He wrote them a letter on March 26, 1901:

The convenient anemometer for field use is the kind with very light flat vanes. The best is made by Richard in Paris (metric units). I have one of them, also a registering instrument graduated to British measure made in Liverpool. Both have been tested and are proved with a formula for corrections. I will lend them, either you like, when you are ready to experiment.

They chose to borrow the Richard anemometer to help them measure wind velocity and calculate the airspeed of their glider.

Richard Anemometer

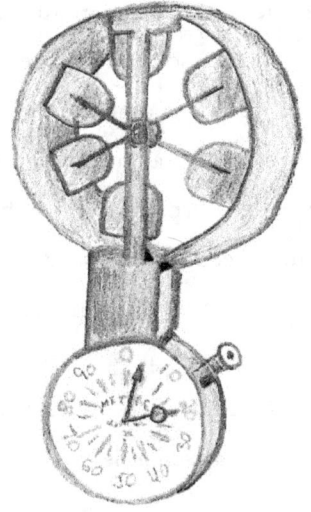

A small lever mounted to your right on the lower wing will start and stop both the stopwatch and the anemometer reading. How can you use these to calculate airspeed and distance traveled?

Under a simple flight one direction, consider

taking a reading of the wind speed into the wind before takeoff. Say the wind is 25 miles per hour toward the nose of the Flyer. Now start your flight and take the reading again during flight. This represents your indicated airspeed – the speed indicated on the Richard anemometer. Can you calculate groundspeed? Sure! Groundspeed is the movement of your Wright Flyer relative to the ground. How about subtracting the wind speed on the Richard anemometer recorded before takeoff from the indicated airspeed during flight? If during flight the anemometer reads 40 miles per hour and the wind coming at you is 25 miles per hour, your groundspeed is: 40 mph – 25 mph (headwind) = 15 mph groundspeed. So, you're traveling along the ground at 15 mph. How about calculating the distance traveled? If you remembered to start the stopwatch when you took flight, you can calculate that also. If the stopwatch reads 30 seconds when you land, then you've traveled:

15 miles/hr x 1hr/60min x 1min/60sec x 30 sec=0.125 miles.

0.125 miles x 5280 ft/mile = **660 feet**

That strong headwind is great for lift, but not

so good for fast travel with only a four-cylinder, 10-15 horsepower four-stroke engine! Now there are some astute pilots out there thinking "But, we use true airspeed and not indicated airspeed in time and distance calculations." Because air becomes less dense with altitude, there are fewer and fewer air molecules hitting the airspeed indicator as the airplane flies higher. With fewer molecules per volume of air turning the vanes of the anemometer in the thinning air at higher altitudes, the indicated airspeed will read inaccurately lower than the true speed of the airplane! A formula to calculate true airspeed corrects for this decreased air density with altitude and will always be higher than the speed indicated on the dial. But let's agree to call the difference between indicated and true airspeed negligible in this case… you're at sea level and will likely be skimming just above the sand dunes and scrub brush!

Lastly, a proper preflight includes checking the fuel level. Look up over your right shoulder. The fuel tank is high up on the wing strut so it can feed the engine by gravity. You have a control near your right hand to open and close the valve supplying fuel to the engine. When you're ready, you can enlist the help of Orville and Wilbur to hand prop the engine. There is only the on-off lever controlling the fuel valve – no throttle! So much for the "power for altitude, pitch for airspeed" mantra! Fly as far as you can and cut the engine to land!

~CHAPTER 4~

CLEARED FOR TAKEOFF!

"The desire to fly is an idea handed down to us by our ancestors who, in their grueling travels across trackless lands in prehistoric times, looked enviously on the birds soaring freely through space, at full speed above all obstacles, on the infinite highway of the air." – Wilbur Wright

As you hang partially over the front of the bottom wing staring at the ground a few feet below your face, you'll notice the Flyer is sitting on a wood rail. It stretches out in front of you about 60 feet. Can you get your Cessna, Cirrus, Piper or Diamond off the ground in 60 feet? The Flyer sits on the rails using a small bicycle wheel hub.

A few things to keep in mind: Your maximum

speed will likely be around 30 mph, just enough to overcome some of those strong gusts! Some sources list the estimated service ceiling of the Wright Flyer as 30 feet. The service ceiling is the height above sea level at which an aircraft is unable to climb faster than a specified rate of climb under standard conditions. For modern aircraft a rate of 100 feet/minute is used. You won't likely be climbing at 100 feet per minute at any altitude in this flying machine… and staying low to the ground is just a good safety tip for your first flight!

While it may be amusing to see the Wright brothers struggling to hand prop the propellers, be kind and remember to open the fuel valve with the stopcock in your right hand before cueing them to bring the engine to life. They may ask you to prime each of the four cylinders with a little fuel to help get it started. Now, get a hold of the elevator lever with your left hand. This will control your pitch – the up and down motion of the Flyer.

Once the engine is running fast and smooth, use your free hand to start the stopwatch and release the restraining rope at the leading edge of the lower wing. Orville and Wilbur can help stabilize the wings while you gain some speed for lift off. Again, amuse yourself by watching them run alongside the Flyer holding the wings steady in their wool suits.

As you start to feel the Flyer get light, pull back slightly on the elevator control with your left hand. This increases the angle of attack of the elevators by raising the front side and lowering the back side. As the air moves faster over the top of the elevator and is directed downward off the trailing edge, the elevators gain lift. This in turn causes the nose of the Flyer to pitch upward and increases the angle of attack on the wings. You suddenly realize just how unstable this very first flying machine is! In an instant, the ground falls away and the horizon starts to pass your view. Even with your neck cricked up that view requires quite an inclination of the machine when you're lying flat on your stomach!

STALL!! STALL!!

As the nose continues to rise, the wing chord line gets to such a large angle with the relative wind direction that the air moving over the top surface becomes turbulent and loses contact with the wing. Remember the critical angle of attack? Well, you've reached it and the wing no longer flies! The only way to regain lift is to reduce that angle of attack below the critical angle again and allow that crisp lifesaving wind to smoothly rush over the airfoil and start magically providing lift again. A word of advice here, however – Do not simply push that elevator control abruptly forward again. Aggressive movement of the flight controls is a bad idea in any aircraft. Forcing the nose abruptly back down could land you straight into the sand dunes. That could lead to some serious injuries and the lifesaving station might not be manned today. Not to mention it's mostly stocked with sailboats and floats. Of course, you'll need a boat and then some to get back to civilization. Worse yet is the scorn of the Wright brothers for breaking their Flyer! Just gently release the back pressure on the elevator control stick in your left hand and let the wings take flight again.

Okay, you've survived that near stall into terrain. Now things feel pretty good! The engine is purring right along, you are straight and level with the horizon, sand, grass and small shrubs rush by about 10 feet below you. Then… as an unstable Flyer is apt to do… the right wing dips.

It is time to get your hips into action. The Wright brothers used the concept of wing warping to control left and right roll or bank of the Flyer. As that right wing dips, move your hips to the left. Cables pull the back of the right wings down while the back of the left wings rise. What happens when the cables pull the back of the wing down? Yep, here we go with angle of attack and lift again! You change the wing chord line to increase the angle of attack on that wing and generate more lift. This causes the wing to rise on that side. This corrects you back to level flight and if held longer starts you into an opposite bank. When turning, the Wright brothers ran into a problem controlling the roll of the earlier glider models of the Flyer. They noticed that when the gliders banked to turn, the high wing experienced greater drag and the nose of the glider would be pulled or 'yaw' in the opposite direction of the turn toward the higher wing. Being a nuanced and astute pilot, Wilbur Wright noted in his diary on August 15, 1901, "Upturned wing seems to fall behind, but at first rises." In some cases, the drag on the higher wing was so severe that the glider would suddenly spin the opposite direction of the turn, stall, and drill down into the sand. They called this "well digging." This drag on the high wing when banking is what we now call "adverse yaw." The tail of the test gliders in 1901 and 1902 had a fixed vertical stabilizer without a rudder. This stabilized the glider in straight flight like the feather on an arrow but did little to correct for the adverse yaw experienced when the glider banked into a turn. They partially solved this in your 1903 Flyer by designing a movable rudder with cables that are physically connected to the wing warping cables and hip cradle. When you move your hips left to bank and turn left, not only does the back of the right wing drop to give you more lift on that side, but the vertical rudders in the back of the Flyer move to the left to help keep the nose from yawing over toward that high wing from the increased drag. In even later designs they disconnected the rudder from the wing-warping movement so it could be controlled separately and provide better coordinated, smoother turns. In the cockpit of modern airplanes, pilots use left and right foot pedals to control the rudder independently of the ailerons. The ailerons serve the same purpose as the wing warping in the Flyer and are controlled by hand using a yoke. No… as fun as it might sound, modern aircraft no longer have hip cradles! The rudder is controlled by foot pedals to counter adverse yaw due to drag of the higher wing allowing execution of smooth, well-coordinated turns. No more well digging!

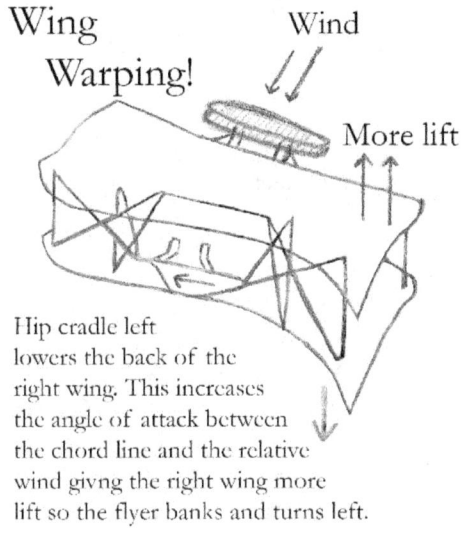

Now, make a few gentle turns in the Flyer. Pushing your hip to the right pulls the rear of the left wing down and the rear of the right wing up. The angle of attack increases on the left wing and decreases on the right wing causing you to bank to the right. The rudder simultaneously hinges to the right slightly helping counter that tendency of the nose to yaw left due to increased wind drag on the raised left wing. Watch your bank angle and don't let it get too steep. Pull out of the turn back to straight and level flight by returning your hips to the middle and removing the wing warp. Also, keep an eye on the horizon! Are you starting to dip forward? Pull back on the elevator control lever ever so slightly to pitch back up. Maybe try to turn back in the other direction now. Push your hip over, watch the bank angle and keep watching that horizon for the pitch! Slow, gentle control movements please!

~CHAPTER 5~

BRING IT HOME

"A good landing is one from which you can walk away. A great landing is one after which they can use the airplane again."

As you turn back toward the takeoff point and the Wright brothers come into view something probably comes to mind. How do I land this thing? Maybe we should have covered that earlier! As the (now old) saying goes, taking off is optional, landing is not!

One major control that modern aircraft possesses and this first Wright Flyer does not is a throttle! Generally, to gain or lose altitude in a controlled fashion, you don't just point the nose up and down. You add power to climb and reduce power to descend. If you tried to climb without sufficient power to overcome the weight of the aircraft, wind over the wings would drop as you slowed to a stall. Then, in properly designed airplanes, the nose would pitch forward and you would start to pick up speed again. Wind would flow back over wings and lift would resume. With sufficient power to climb, airspeed is maintained, wind flows over the wings and the airplane ascends. How about the descent? If you descend by simply pointing the nose down with full power plus the added help of gravity, the aircraft will continue to pick up airspeed as it plummets toward earth. Then, to avoid crashing nose first into a sand dune, you might pull that elevator stick back. Can't land now! As you start to level out, the wings fully utilize all that airspeed from the rushing wind, regain lift, and you simply start flying again! Well remember, the Wright Flyer you are now floating across the sand in doesn't have a throttle control – fuel is either full on with maximum engine thrust or full off with no power at all! Fortunately, you are not looking for some far-off runway and are not cruising over a metropolitan jungle of houses and buildings. Just avoid rising sand dunes and trees, find a clearing, then reach up over your head on the right and shut off the fuel line stopcock beneath the 4-gallon fuel tank. The engine quits, the propellers stop rotating, you start losing airspeed and the wings lose their lift.

Avoid pointing the nose down as you lose that lift. Think of how a seagull lands. It slows down, lifts his head in a perfect stall and lands gently on its feet. Birds… they make it look so easy! As the sand rushes up toward your face, keep some back pressure on that elevator stick to keep the nose up just enough to slow you down and gently touch back down to earth. Some call this flaring the nose or "the flare" on landing. But do not flare up so much or so early that the Flyer stalls nose high and drops out of the sky! That could be jarring! Don't forget to use your hips to keep those wings level and stay flying straight ahead as you land so you don't hit a wing tip first and cartwheel. Don't get lazy now! Concentrate and fly it all the way until you are stopped again on the sand of Kill Devil Hills. And stay away from the ocean… remember, you're flying the first and only working, heavier-than-air, controlled flying machine in the entire world in 1903!

Orville and Wilbur run up to greet you and congratulate you on a fantastic flight in the first Wright Flyer. Maybe you've planted the seed for their flight school. They started it in an old cotton field in Montgomery, Alabama seven years later in 1910. It will cost about $500 to train with them, but there will be a "no-charge" policy for damaging the airplane!

Now don't you want to go flying again?

"When once you have tasted flight you will forever walk the earth with your eyes turned skyward, for there you have been, and there you will always long to return" – Leonardo DaVinci

EPILOGUE

The Wrights continued working on their flying machines after the historic first flight in 1903. From a practical standpoint they obtained permission to start flying in a local cow pasture known as Huffman Prairie, a few miles outside of Dayton, Ohio. Given you lay face down without substantial landing gear in the Wright Flyer, I'm guessing our flying adventure in the sand dunes of Kitty Hawk, N.C. with a fresh ocean breeze was more desirable than in a manure laden field in Ohio!

The second powered Flyer built in 1904 was almost a complete copy of the first model and they did not achieve another flight longer than the 59 second flight of 1903 until their 49th flight of the new model. While in our flight today you returned to the point of takeoff, in reality it wasn't until almost a year later on October 20, 1904, that the Wrights flew a complete circle. The flight lasted 1 minute and 36 seconds and covered 4,080 feet.

Real improvements came in the 1905 Flyer. They made the canard style elevator and the rudders larger in the front and back giving the pilot more authority over pitch (up and down) and yaw (left and right) of the aircraft. Some semicircular "blinkers" between the elevator surfaces helped prevent the nose from dipping and the Flyer from slipping sideways during turns. They were also able to make some small improvements to the propellers to help with thrust. Even with some of these improvements, flying was still a dangerous proposition! On July 14th, 1905, Orville had a serious crash that threw him through the top wing and destroyed the front elevator!

To gain even more flight control, they moved the elevator out from 7 ½ feet to 12 feet beyond the wings and extended the rudder out as well. They also made new propellers with a slightly bent end to help prevent them from flattening out and losing thrust.

These improvements helped immensely! In August, about a month and a half after Orville's nearly fatal crash, they were flying multiple circles around the pasture and landing reliably. On September 26th, Wilber ran the fuel tank dry after being airborne for almost 20 minutes! Unfortunately, that is a common and often devastating mistake many a pilot still makes today!

The word spread and people often showed up to watch them fly the more stable 1905 Flyer. It was taking off, ascending, descending, turning and landing under full control of the pilot for long periods of time without causing damage or injuries – a real functioning airplane! However, the publicity garnered some concern among the Wright brothers. Stories started to appear in the local newspapers, and they had not secured all of their patents. They subsequently did not fly again until 1907.

From 1907 until 1909 the Wrights built the Wright Model A. It was the world's first production model airplane. It was based on the 1905 Flyer III with some improvements. It was longer and had a more powerful engine. It could carry more weight so they added two seats on the leading edge of the wing. Sitting upright seems like a much more natural, comfortable and safer way to fly an airplane and carry a passenger! The new Flyer also allowed the pilot to control the three dimensions of flight separately – unique controls for turning (wing warping), pitch (elevator) and yaw (rudder). Remember, the first Flyers countered adverse yaw in turns due to increased drag on the high wing by connecting rudder control to the wing warping. Interestingly, Wilber and Orville preferred slightly different control designs. Airplanes manufactured in Europe mostly had the system designed by Wilbur while those in America mostly had the system designed by Orville. Orville's build used three levers. Moving a middle lever between the seats forward and backward warped the wings to control roll/banking. This forward-backward movement seems counterintuitive given warping the wings turns the airplane left and right! A small lever on top of this middle lever twisted to adjust the rudder, which modern pilots control using foot pedals. So, turning left would require moving the middle lever forward and twisting it slightly to adjust for adverse yaw. The outside levers controlled the elevator to pitch the nose up and down. Wilbur tried to simplify this a bit by having the wing warping lever move forward and backward to control bank and left and right to control the rudder in the single control. A second lever to the left controlled the elevator for pitch.

  The end of 1909 also brought an end to the Model A Flyer. The Wrights had started to add a fixed horizontal stabilizer more akin to the modern airplane tail to the back of the aircraft near the rudder. This evolved into a movable elevator at the tail requiring a sturdier frame. By 1910 the canard style elevator in the front had been completely phased out and the Model A was replaced with the Model B lovingly nicknamed the "headless Wright"! This model had an even longer rudder and elevator length and added wheels.

Increasingly better versions of the 1910 Model B were produced through 1914 at which time the "pusher" design with propellers positioned in the back was deemed less stable and more dangerous. As such, it started losing its share of the market. The 1915 Wright Model K was their first airplane with the engine in front of the wings to pull the airplane through the air "tractor style." It was built for the United States Navy as a seaplane! The Wright Company manufactured its last aircraft for the army in 1916 – the 1916 Wright Model L. By that time, Wilbur had died, and Orville was less involved in the aircraft design.

Wilbur Wright died in Dayton on May 30, 1912 of typhoid at the age of 45.

Orville Wright died January 30, 1948 at the age of 76. After his brother died of typhoid, he held the Wright Company on his own for a few years, selling it on October 15, 1915 to investors for a reported $1.5

million. A year later it merged with the Glenn L. Martin Company to become the Wright-Martin Company. This company only existed a couple of years before Martin resigned. The Wright-Martin joint venture dissolved and reemerged as Wright Aeronautical in 1919. They switched from manufacturing aircraft to primarily making aircraft engines. Glenn Martin continued with his main company to remain a major manufacturer of aircraft and eventually rockets for missiles and spacecraft. The company merged with American-Marietta Corporation in 1961 to become Martin-Marietta, which then merged again with Lockheed in 1995 to become Lockheed-Martin!

1903 FLYER SPECIFICATIONS

Component	Specification	Notes
Length	21 feet	
Wingspan	40 feet 4 inches	Right wing was 4 inches longer to compensate for the engine weight.
Wing chord	6 feet 6 inches	
Wing anhedral	10 inches	Wing droop
Wing surface area	510 square feet	All wings
Elevator surface area	48 square feet	Both surfaces

Rudder surface area	20 square feet	Both surfaces
Weight without fuel	605 pounds	
Fluid weights	16 pounds	Gas, oil and water
Engine	4 cylinders	
	4-cycle gasoline	
	4-inch bore	
	4-inch stroke	
	Aluminum-copper alloy crankcase	
	12 HP at 1020 RPM	
	152 pounds	
	Gravity fed fuel	
	Thermo-siphon water radiator for cooling	
	Splash and dash lubrication activated by the crankshaft	
	~980 RPM in flight	
Ignition	Start with dry batteries and switch to magneto	
Propellers	Twin propellers	

rotating opposite directions
Push configuration
Driven by the engine using a 1 inch roller chain
8-tooth sprockets on the crankshaft
22-tooth sprockets on the propeller shafts
2-7/8:1 Engine to propeller RPM ratio
~340 RPM in flight

GLOSSARY

Absolute altitude. The vertical distance of an airplane above the terrain or above ground level (AGL).

Adverse yaw. A condition of flight in which the nose of an airplane tends to move (yaw) toward the outside of the turn. This is caused by the higher induced drag on the outside wing, which is also producing more lift. Induced drag is a by-product of the lift associated with the outside wing.

Ailerons. Primary flight control surfaces mounted on the trailing edge of an airplane wing, near the tip. Ailerons control roll about the longitudinal axis. They took the place of the Wright's wing warping box.

Airfoil. An airfoil is any surface, such as a wing, propeller, rudder, or even a trim tab, which provides aerodynamic force when it interacts with a moving stream of air.

Altimeter. A flight instrument that indicates altitude by sensing pressure changes.

Altitude (AGL). The actual height above ground level (AGL) at which the aircraft is flying.

Altitude (MSL). The actual height above mean sea level (MSL) at which the aircraft is flying.

Angle of attack. The acute angle between the chord line (line from the leading edge to the trailing edge of the wing) of the airfoil and the direction of the relative wind (wind coming toward the airfoil (wing)).

Attitude indicator. An instrument which uses an artificial horizon and miniature airplane to depict the position of the airplane in relation to the true horizon. The attitude indicator senses roll as well as pitch, which is the up and down movement of the airplane's nose.

Attitude. The position of an aircraft as determined by the relationship of its axes and a reference, usually the earth's horizon.

Axes of an aircraft. Three imaginary lines that pass through an aircraft's center of gravity. The axes can be considered as imaginary axles around which the aircraft turns. The three axes pass through the center of gravity at 90° angles to each other. The axis from nose to tail is the longitudinal axis, the axis that passes from wingtip to wingtip is the lateral axis, and the axis that passes vertically through the center of gravity is the vertical axis.

Chord line. An imaginary straight line drawn through an airfoil (wing) from the leading edge to the trailing edge.

Coordinated flight. Application of all appropriate flight and power controls to prevent slipping or skidding in any flight condition.

Crab. A flight condition in which the nose of the airplane is pointed into the wind a sufficient amount to counteract a crosswind and maintain a desired track over the ground.

Critical angle of attack. The angle of attack at which a wing stalls regardless of airspeed, flight attitude, or weight.

Crosswind component. The wind component, measured in knots, at 90° to the longitudinal axis of the runway.

Density altitude. This altitude is pressure altitude corrected for variations from standard temperature. When conditions are standard, pressure altitude and density altitude are the same. If the temperature is above standard, the density altitude is higher than pressure altitude. If the temperature is below standard, the density altitude is lower than pressure altitude. This is an important altitude because it is directly related to the airplane's performance.

Ditching. Emergency landing in water.

Downwash. Air deflected perpendicular to the motion of the airfoil.

Elevator. The horizontal, movable primary control surface in the tail section, or empennage, of an airplane. The elevator is hinged to the trailing edge of the fixed horizontal stabilizer. It controls pitch up or down of the nose along the lateral axis.

Empennage. The section of the airplane that consists of the vertical stabilizer, the horizontal stabilizer, and the associated control surfaces.

Fuselage. The section of the airplane that consists of the cabin and/or cockpit, containing seats for the occupants and the controls for the airplane.

Groundspeed (GS). The actual speed of the airplane over the ground. It is true airspeed adjusted for wind. Groundspeed decreases with a headwind, and increases with a tailwind.

Gyroscopic precession. An inherent quality of rotating bodies, which causes an applied force to be manifested 90° in the direction of rotation from the point where the force is applied.

Hand propping. Starting an engine by rotating the

propeller by hand.

Heading. The direction in which the nose of the aircraft is pointing during flight.

Headwind component. The component of atmospheric winds that acts opposite to the aircraft's flightpath.

Horizon. The line-of-sight boundary between the earth and the sky.

Horsepower. The term, originated by inventor James Watt, means the amount of work a horse could do in one second. One horsepower equals 550 foot-pounds per second, or 33,000 foot-pounds per minute.

Indicated airspeed (IAS). The direct instrument reading obtained from the airspeed indicator, uncorrected for variations in atmospheric density, installation error, or instrument error. Manufacturers use this airspeed as the basis for determining airplane performance. Takeoff, landing, and stall speeds listed in the airplane flight manual or pilots operating handbook are indicated airspeeds and do not normally vary with altitude or temperature.

Indicated altitude. The altitude read directly from the altimeter (uncorrected) when it is set to the current altimeter setting.

Induced drag. That part of total drag which is created by the production of lift. Induced drag increases with a decrease in airspeed.

Initial climb. This stage of the climb begins when the airplane leaves the ground and a pitch attitude has been established to climb away from the takeoff area.

Instrument Flight Rules (IFR). Rules that govern the procedure for conducting flight in weather conditions below VFR weather minimums. The term "IFR" also is used to define weather conditions and the type of flight plan under which an aircraft is operating.

International Standard Atmosphere (ISA). Standard atmospheric conditions consisting of a temperature of 59 °F (15 °C), and a barometric pressure of 29.92 "Hg. (1013.2 mb) at sea level. ISA values can be calculated for various altitudes using a standard lapse rate of approximately 2 °C per 1,000 feet.

Lateral axis. An imaginary line passing through the center of gravity of an airplane and extending across the airplane from wingtip to wingtip.

Leading edge. The part of an airfoil that meets the airflow first.

Lift coefficient. A coefficient representing the lift of a given airfoil. Lift coefficient is obtained by dividing the lift by the free-stream dynamic pressure and the representative area under consideration.

Lift. One of the four main forces acting on an aircraft. On a fixed-wing aircraft, an upward force created by the effect of airflow as it passes over and under the wing.

Lift/drag ratio (L/D). The efficiency of an airfoil section. It is the ratio of the coefficient of lift to the coefficient of drag for any given angle of attack.

Longitudinal axis. An imaginary line through an aircraft from nose to tail, passing through its center of gravity. The longitudinal axis is also called the roll axis of the aircraft. Movement of the ailerons or wing warping rotates an airplane about its longitudinal axis.

Parasite drag. That part of total drag created by the design or shape of airplane parts. Parasite drag increases with an increase in airspeed.

P-factor. A tendency for an aircraft to yaw to the left due to the descending propeller blade on the right producing more thrust than the ascending blade on the left. This occurs when the aircraft's longitudinal axis is in a climbing attitude in relation to the relative wind. The P-factor would be to the right if the aircraft had a counterclockwise rotating propeller. The Wright Flyer had two propellers rotating opposite directions helping to counteract this force.

Pitch. The rotation of an airplane about its lateral axis, or on a propeller, the blade angle as measured from airplane of rotation. It refers to the up and down motion of the nose.

Pressure altitude. The altitude indicated when the altimeter setting window (barometric scale) is adjusted to 29.92. This is the altitude above the standard datum airplane, which is a theoretical airplane where air pressure (corrected to 15 °C) equals 29.92 "Hg. Pressure altitude is used to compute density altitude, true altitude, true airspeed, and other performance data.

Propeller. A device for propelling an aircraft that, when rotated, produces by its action on the air, a thrust approximately perpendicular to its airplane of rotation. It includes the control components normally supplied by its manufacturer.

Reciprocating engine. An engine that converts the heat energy from burning fuel into the reciprocating movement of the pistons. This movement is converted into a rotary motion by the connecting rods and crankshaft.

Relative wind. The direction of the airflow with respect to the wing. If a wing moves forward horizontally, the relative wind moves backward horizontally. Relative wind is parallel to and opposite the flightpath of the airplane.

Roll. The motion of the aircraft about the longitudinal axis. It is controlled by the ailerons in modern aircraft and by wing warping in the Wright Flyer.

Rudder. The movable primary control surface mounted on the trailing edge of the vertical fin of an airplane. Movement of the rudder rotates the airplane about its vertical axis causing the airplane to yaw.

Sea level. A reference height used to determine standard atmospheric conditions and altitude measurements.

Service ceiling. The maximum density altitude where the best rate-of-climb airspeed will produce a 100 feet-per-minute climb at maximum weight while in a clean configuration with maximum continuous power.

Skid. A condition where the tail of the airplane follows a path outside the path of the nose during a turn.

Slip. An intentional maneuver to decrease airspeed or increase rate of descent, and to compensate for a crosswind on landing. A slip can also be unintentional when the pilot fails to maintain the aircraft in coordinated flight.

Stability. The inherent quality of an airplane to correct for conditions that may disturb its equilibrium, and to return or to continue on the original flightpath. It is primarily an airplane design characteristic.

Stall. A rapid decrease in lift caused by the separation of airflow from the wing's surface brought on by exceeding the critical angle of attack. A stall can occur at any pitch attitude or airspeed.

Standard atmosphere. At sea level, the standard atmosphere consists of a barometric pressure of 29.92 inches of mercury ("Hg) or 1013.2 millibars, and a temperature of 15 °C (59 °F). Pressure and temperature normally decrease as altitude increases. The standard lapse rate in the lower atmosphere for each 1,000 feet of altitude is approximately 1 "Hg and 2 °C (3.5 °F). For example, the standard pressure and temperature at 3,000 feet mean sea level (MSL) is 26.92 "Hg (29.92 – 3) and 9 °C (15 °C – 6 °C).

Takeoff roll (ground roll). The total distance required for an aircraft to become airborne.

Throttle. The valve in a carburetor or fuel control unit that determines the amount of fuel-air mixture that is fed to the engine.

Thrust. The force which imparts a change in the velocity of a mass. This force is measured in pounds but has no element of time or rate. A forward force which propels the airplane through the air.

Total drag. The sum of the parasite and induced drag.

True airspeed (TAS). Calibrated airspeed corrected for altitude and nonstandard temperature. Because air density decreases with an increase in altitude, an airplane has to be flown faster at higher altitudes to cause the same pressure difference between pitot impact pressure and static pressure. Therefore, for a given calibrated airspeed, true airspeed increases as altitude increases; or for a given true airspeed, calibrated airspeed decreases as altitude increases.

True altitude. The vertical distance of the airplane above sea level—the actual altitude. It is often expressed as feet above mean sea level (MSL). Airport, terrain, and obstacle elevations on aeronautical charts are true altitudes.

Useful load. The weight of the pilot, copilot, passengers, baggage, usable fuel, and drainable oil. It is the basic empty weight subtracted from the maximum allowable gross weight. This term applies to general aviation aircraft only.

Velocity. The speed or rate of movement in a certain direction.

Vertical axis. An imaginary line passing vertically through the center of gravity of an aircraft. The vertical axis is called the z-axis or the yaw axis.

Vertical stability. Stability about an aircraft's vertical axis. Also called yawing or directional stability.

Visual Flight Rules (VFR). Code of Federal Regulations that govern the procedures for conducting flight under visual conditions.

Weathervane. The tendency of the aircraft to turn into the relative wind.

Weight and balance. The aircraft is said to be in

weight and balance when the gross weight of the aircraft is under the max gross weight, and the center of gravity is within limits and will remain in limits for the duration of the flight.

Weight. A measure of the heaviness of an object. The force by which a body is attracted toward the center of the earth (or another celestial body) by gravity. Weight is equal to the mass of the body times the local value of gravitational acceleration. One of the four main forces acting on an aircraft. Equivalent to the actual weight of the aircraft. It acts downward through the aircraft's center of gravity toward the center of the earth. Weight opposes lift.

Wind correction angle. Correction applied to the course to establish a heading so that track will coincide with course.

Wing. Airfoil attached to each side of the fuselage and are the main lifting surfaces that support the airplane in flight.

Wing area. The total surface of the wing (square feet), which includes control surfaces and may include wing area covered by the fuselage (main body of the airplane), and engine nacelles.

Wing span. The maximum distance from wingtip to wingtip.

Yaw. Rotation about the vertical axis of an aircraft.

ACKNOWLEDGEMENTS

Thank you to Colette and Jeremy for their critical review, suggestions, and proofreading!

ABOUT THE AUTHOR

Christopher Felten is a physician and private pilot in Los Angeles. His home airport is KVNY. He considers himself a "serial enthusiast" and when not working or flying enjoys playing trombone with wind ensembles and big bands, surfing, amateur radio, running and spending time with family.

www.ingramcontent.com/pod-product-compliance
Lightning Source LLC
Chambersburg PA
CBHW070742060526
44119CB00071B/115